Bread

by **Dana Meachen Rau**

Reading Consultant: Nanci R. Vargus, Ed.D.

Marshall Cavendish
Benchmark
New York

Picture Words

 bread

 butter

 cheese

knife

 loaf

 sandwich

soup

 can be white.

 can be tall.

 can be brown.

 can be small.

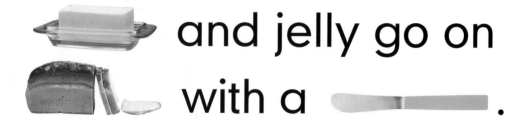 and jelly go on with a ———.

12

We take a  and cut a slice.

 with  is very nice.

We add two slices of to and meat.

A  is so good
to eat!

Words to Know

sandwich (SAN-dwich)
  two slices of bread with other
  foods in between

slices
  pieces of bread

Find Out More

Books

Anderson, Catherine. *Bread Bakery*. Chicago, IL: Heinemann Library, 2005.

Thoennes Keller, Kristin. *From Wheat to Bread*. Mankato, MN: Capstone Press, 2004.

Videos

Raider, Stacey. *Reading Rainbow: Bread Is for Eating*. Lincoln, Nebraska: GPN.

Sands, Brinna. *Breadtime Tales*. Huntington, NY: Kelvin 5400, Inc.

Web Sites

Child Fun: Bread Activities
www.holsumaz.com/Just_For_Kids/How_to_Make_ Bread.php

Kids Health Recipes: Pretzels
www.kidshealth.org/kid/recipes/recipes/pretzel.html

USDA: MyPyramid.gov
www.mypyramid.gov/kids/index.html

About the Author

Dana Meachen Rau is an author, editor, and illustrator. A graduate of Trinity College in Hartford, Connecticut, she has written more than two hundred books for children, including nonfiction, biographies, early readers, and historical fiction. She likes to bake bread with her family in Burlington, Connecticut.

About the Reading Consultant

Nanci R. Vargus, Ed.D., wants all children to enjoy reading. She used to teach first grade. Now she works at the University of Indianapolis. Nanci helps young people become teachers. She would rather eat bread than bake it!

Marshall Cavendish Benchmark
99 White Plains Road
Tarrytown, NY 10591-5502
www.marshallcavendish.us

Copyright © 2009 by Marshall Cavendish Corporation

All Internet addresses were correct at the time of printing.

Library of Congress Cataloging-in-Publication Data
Rau, Dana Meachen, 1971–
Bread / by Dana Meachen Rau.
    p. cm. — (Benchmark Rebus : What's Cooking?)
Summary: "Easy to read text with rebuses explores different varieties of bread"—Provided by publisher.
Includes bibliographical references.
ISBN 978-0-7614-2892-3
1. Bread—Juvenile literature. I. Title.
TX769.R34 2008
641.8'15--dc22
      2007021876

Editor: Christine Florie
Publisher: Michelle Bisson
Art Director: Anahid Hamparian
Series Designer: Virginia Pope

Photo research by Connie Gardner

Rebus images, with the exception of sandwich, provided courtesy of *Dorling Kindersley*.

Cover photo by Sky Bonillo/*PhotoEdit*

The photographs in this book are used with the permission and through the courtesy of:
Envision/Corbis: p. 3 (sandwich); *Corbis*: p. 5 peace/amana; p. 11 Joe Bator; p. 15 A. Inden/zefa; p. 19 Chuck Savage; p. 21 LWA-Stephen Welstead; *Getty Images*: pp. 7, 9 Marc Grimber; p. 17 Hans Carien; *Jupiter Images*: p. 13 Francis Hammond.

Printed in Malaysia
1 3 5 6 4 2